SandCastle™

Mini Animal Marvels

Miniature Farm Animals

A Division of ABDO

ABDO
Publishing Company

Alex Kuskowski   Consulting Editor, Diane Craig, M.A./Reading Specialist

visit us at www.abdopublishing.com

Published by ABDO Publishing Company, a division of ABDO, P.O. Box 398166, Minneapolis, Minnesota 55439. Copyright © 2014 by Abdo Consulting Group, Inc. International copyrights reserved in all countries. No part of this book may be reproduced in any form without written permission from the publisher. SandCastle™ is a trademark and logo of ABDO Publishing Company.

Printed in the United States of America, North Mankato, Minnesota
102013
012014

Editor: Liz Salzmann
Content Developer: Alex Kuskowski
Cover and Interior Design and Production: Mighty Media, Inc.
Photo Credits: Shutterstock

Library of Congress Cataloging-in-Publication Data

Kuskowski, Alex.
  Miniature farm animals / Alex Kuskowski.
     pages cm. -- (Mini animal marvels)
  ISBN 978-1-62403-066-6
1. Domestic animals--Juvenile fiction. 2. Domestic animals--Size. I. Title.
  SF75.5.K875 2014
  636--dc23
                         2013022906

SandCastle™ Level: Transitional

SandCastle™ books are created by a team of professional educators, reading specialists, and content developers around five essential components—phonemic awareness, phonics, vocabulary, text comprehension, and fluency—to assist young readers as they develop reading skills and strategies and increase their general knowledge. All books are written, reviewed, and leveled for guided reading, early reading intervention, and Accelerated Reader® programs for use in shared, guided, and independent reading and writing activities to support a balanced approach to literacy instruction. The SandCastle™ series has four levels that correspond to early literacy development. The levels are provided to help teachers and parents select appropriate books for young readers.

| Emerging Readers (no flags) | Beginning Readers (1 flag) | Transitional Readers (2 flags) | Fluent Readers (3 flags) |

Table of Contents

Miniature Farm Animals

Miniature farm animals are small animals living on farms. Some can do farm work. Some are pets.

Miniature Cow

Miniature cows are the smallest cows. They live on farms all over the world.

It is 46 inches
(116.8 cm) tall.

6 feet
(1.8 m)

46 inches
(116.8 cm)

Farmers keep miniature cows for milk. Each cow can make 4 **gallons** (15 L) of milk a day!

Miniature Pig

The miniature pig is a small pig. People keep them as pets. The pigs are playful.

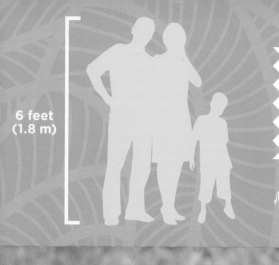

**6 feet
(1.8 m)**

It is 16 inches
(40.6 cm) tall.

**16 inches
(40.6 cm)**

Miniature pigs like to eat. They stick their noses into their food.

The pigs live in a group.
They play together.

Miniature Goat

Miniature goats are small goats. They are **tough**. They can live anywhere.

6 feet
(1.8 m)

It is 20 inches
(50.8 cm) tall.

20 inches
(50.8 cm)

Miniature goats eat plants.
They sleep on hay.

Miniature goats live together.
They play together too.

Miniature Horse

A miniature horse is a small horse. It is the same size as a small pony.

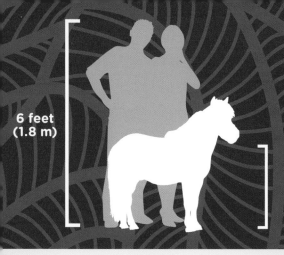

6 feet
(1.8 m)

34 inches
(86.4 cm)

It is 34 inches
(86.4 cm) tall.

Miniature horses play outside. They **gallop** across fields. They eat grass and hay.

Did You Know?

 Cows have 32 teeth.

 Pigs have four toes.

 Miniature goats have **horizontal pupils.**

 A horse's teeth never stop growing.

Farm Animal Quiz

1   Farmers don't get milk from miniature cows.

2   Miniature pigs stick their noses into their food.

3   Miniature goats are not **tough**.

4   Miniature goats live alone.

5   A miniature horse is the same size as a small pony.

Answers: 1. False 2. True 3. False 4. False 5. True

Glossary

gallon – a unit for measuring liquids. Milk and gasoline are often sold by the gallon.

gallop – to run fast so that all four feet are off the ground at the same time once in each stride.

horizontal – in the same direction as the ground, or side-to-side.

pupil – the black center of an eye.

tough – able to survive difficult conditions.